Contents

everything

early years

Introduction

Thinking of things to make and do with young babies can be a struggle for child carers. The range of equipment for this age-group always seems to consist of the same items, and, after a while, both carer and baby can become bored of the same old rattles. This book provides you with a range of items that you can make very simply and without much expense. It also suggests ways to play with and explore these items to cover certain aspects of the **Birth to Three** Framework. Each resource covers more than one area – and how you decide to play with the item will determine what aspect you cover.

As a parent or practitioner your role is to provide appropriate activities and resources to assist a child in discovering and developing within a safe and caring environment. If you make regular observations of your child you will know how and when to extend the activities to offer more learning opportunities. Remember each child will develop at his/her own rate and no 2 children are exactly the same.

Safety can be an area of concern when making your own equipment. When making and playing with any of the resources in this book please ensure you use appropriate materials, and that babies and young children are supervised at all times.

The resources included in this book are primarily aimed at the *Heads Up, Lookers and Communicators* (0–8 months) and *Sitters, Standers and Explorers* (8–18 months) age-groups specified in the **Birth to Three Matters** Framework as set out by the DFES and Sure Start. However, there are ideas included on how to extend the activity to cover the *Movers, Shakers and Players* (18–24 months) and *Walkers, Talkers and Pretenders* (24–36 months) age-groups.

Links to Birth to Three Matters

The chart on page 3 clearly shows how the resources in this book can be used to link into **Birth to 3 Matters**. As soon as an updated version of the Framework appears we will put a free chart on our website showing how the resources match this. Please go to www.everythingearlyyears.co.uk.

Aspects	Components			
A Strong Child	**Me, Myself and I** *Awareness of self* 3* *Finding out what he/she can do* 4, 7, 10, 12 *Recognising personal characteristics* 6	**Being Acknowledged and Affirmed** *Exploring emotional boundaries* 11	**Developing Self-assurance** *Becoming confident in what he/she can do* 4, 7, 10, 12	**A Sense of Belonging** *Being able to snuggle in* 3, 6, 8 *Enjoying being with familiar and trusted others* 6, 8, 9, 12, 13, 14
A Skilful Communicator	**Being Together** *Being with others* 3, 8, 11, 13 *Positive relationships* 3, 8, 11, 13 *Gaining attention and making contact* 8, 11, 13 *Encouraging conversation* 8, 11, 13, 14	**Finding a Voice** *The impulse to communicate* 8, 11, 13, 14 *Exploring, experimenting, labelling and expressing* 8, 13, 14	**Listening and Responding** *Enjoying and sharing stories, songs, rhymes and games* 5, 8, 11, 13 *Listening and paying attention to what others say* 8, 11, 13, 14 *Learning about words and meanings* 8, 13, 14 *Making playful and serious responses* 8, 11, 13	**Making Meaning** *Understanding each other* 3, 8, 11, 13
A Competent Learner	**Making Connections** *Making connections through the senses and movement* 1, 6, 12 *Becoming playfully engaged and involved* 1, 2, 4, 6, 7, 8, 9, 10, 11, 12, 13, 14 *Finding out about the environment and other people* 8, 13	**Being Imaginative** *Playing imaginatively with materials using all the senses* 3, 4 *Exploring and re-enacting* 4	**Being Creative** *Exploring and discovering* 2, 3, 4, 5, 7, 9, 10, 13, 14 *Experimenting with sound, other media and movement* 5, 9	**Representing** *Creating and experimenting with one's own symbols and marks* 8, 13
A Healthy Child	**Emotional Well-being** *Developing healthy independence* 4, 13	**Growing and Developing** *Being active, rested and protected* 2, 10, 12, 14 *Gaining control of the body* 2, 4, 5, 7, 9, 10, 11, 12, 13, 14 *Acquiring physical skills* 4, 5, 7, 9, 10, 11, 12, 13, 14	**Keeping Safe** *Learning about rules* 11 *Knowing when and how to ask for help* 11	**Healthy Choices** *Making decisions* 2, 7 *Demonstrating individual preferences* 2, 6 *Discovering and learning about his/her body* 1

* Resource reference

everything
early years

Mobiles

Babies do not need expensive shop bought mobiles. Young babies can only focus at short distances and are interested in bright bold patterns. In fact, very young babies can only see in red, black and white, so these are good colours to use when creating your mobile.

When hanging mobiles you need to ensure that they are close enough for the baby to focus on, but just out of reach – so there is no risk of the baby getting caught up in the strings, ribbons or items attached. The best places to hang mobiles are above changing units, cots or bouncy chairs. Another good place to hang them is in a window or a door way. When the door or window is open the mobile will gently move in the wind, and when it is closed the sunlight will make interesting shadows and reflections to look at.

What you need

- Coloured string, cotton, wool or thread to hang your items.
- Brightly coloured card to cut out shapes from.
- Black, white and red paint.
- Pictures or light weight items to hang from your mobile.
- Ribbon to hang in strips from your mobile.
- Stiff card or thin wood to make the shape to hang the items from.
- Hole punch or a thick blunt needle to make holes in your pictures and shapes to hang them.
- Small bells to attach to the mobile to make noise when it moves in the wind.

Making your mobile

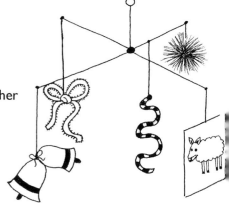

- Using the template provided, trace and cut out two of these shapes onto strong card.
- Where marked on the pattern, make the small holes and slit – using either a hole punch or a blunt needle and scissors. Slot the 2 pieces together.
- You can now attach the coloured thread, wool or cotton – it is a good idea to vary the length of these, the one in the middle should be the longest or shortest piece of thread.
- You are now ready to hang your pictures, ribbons and other items.

What to do next

Heads Up, Lookers and Communicators and *Sitters, Standers and Explorers*

Hang your mobile where the baby can clearly see it. If you place it in a window the items will move in the breeze and may also make interesting shadows for the baby to look at.

Movers, Shakers and Players and *Walkers, Talkers and Pretenders*

It can be a good idea to hang the mobile over the changing unit and use items or pictures the child is familiar with. Take the time when changing the child to recognise and name the items. You could use pictures of animals and teach the child the noises they make, or pictures of body parts and ask the child to point to their own eyes, nose, feet and so on.

everything

Shake and see bottles

Babies of all ages and stages of development love these bottles – and they are very easy to make. Before you know it you will have a collection of exciting bottles for the babies to play with. A particularly good thing about this resource is that if you are making bottles in your setting then, before long, parents will copy your ideas at home and begin to tell you about different materials they have used. Or they may begin collecting empty bottles for you!

An important thing to take into consideration when making these, is that you use appropriate sizes and that the bottles are transparent.

What you need

- A range of empty plastic bottles with their lids – small water bottles are very good to use for the younger baby.

- Super glue to secure the lids once items are inside.

- A range of items to place in the bottle, these could include: different coloured buttons, lentils, coloured rice and pasta, feathers, bottle tops, different coloured water, tinsel or shiny paper, sequins, nuts and bolts.

- A funnel.

Making your bottles

- Once you have decided which items to place in your bottles, soak off the labels and place the items inside. You may need to use a funnel to help pour smaller items into the neck of the bottle. Sequins and water work well together.

- Take into consideration how heavy the items are, and do not over fill the bottle. The babies need to be able to pick up the bottles and there has to be space left in the bottle to shake and move the items around.

- Once you have the items inside the bottle you need to glue the lid shut so that it can't be opened. Leave this to dry completely before allowing the baby to play with it.

- You could hang them with string on a fence outside, these can be fun to play with.

  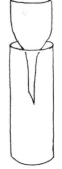 

What to do next

Heads Up, Lookers and Communicators and *Sitters, Standers and Explorers*

You are now ready to play with the bottles. Allow the baby to explore the bottles for themselves. Show the baby what happens when you shake or roll the bottles along the ground, hold the bottles up to the light for them to look through. Make sure you have a range of bottles – which are both heavy and light.

Movers, Shakers and Players and *Walkers, Talkers and Pretenders*

Involve the older age-groups with the making of the bottles – offering them a choice of what to add. Use descriptive words when they are playing, for example: shaking, rolling, heavy and light. You can also encourage this age-group to pick up the bottles and shake them in time to their favourite nursery rhymes.

everything
early years

Feely bags

Feely bags are a lovely way for babies to explore and experience a sense of touch. By using a range of materials babies will be able to experience different textures, colours and even noises. When choosing the materials to use in your feely bags please make sure that you are going to be able to wash or sponge the materials clean if needed. In addition, try and use a range of natural and man-made materials.

What you need

- Pillowcase.
- Ribbon.
- Needle and thread.
- A range of materials, for example: cotton canvas, rubber, voile, fake fur, corduroy, PVC, silk, satin, lace, lycra, ribbon, shiny sequin material, sheets of sandpaper.

Making your feely bags

- Cut the material into different sized pieces, making sure that they are manageable for the babies you are caring for. Some material may be likely to fray, if this is the case you may need to edge it. This can be done by either tacking a hem around the edge of the material or using wonder webbing and ironing the open edges over.

- You will also need to make a bag to keep all your pieces of material in, you can use an old pillow case for this. Fold over the top and make a channel by stitching around the top, leaving an opening to thread some ribbon through to make this a draw-string bag. Keep the bag out of reach of babies as the draw-string can be dangerous.

What to do next

Heads Up, Lookers and Communicators and *Sitters, Standers and Explorers*

When you are playing with the feely bag, encourage the baby to stroke and touch the different materials. Try gently rubbing the material on their cheek, or remove their shoes and socks, and rub the material gently over the soles of their feet. Cover some other toys using the pieces of material and encourage the baby to lift the material and look underneath. Snuggle the baby up in some of the cosier material and have a cuddle.

Movers, Shakers and Players and *Walkers, Talkers and Pretenders*

Once again, use this to snuggle the child up in, but you can also encourage the child to walk or crawl on the material to feel the texture. You can also introduce descriptive words when feeling the texture of the material. Hang the material over equipment, making a hiding place for the child to play in. Wrap a doll in the material or use it as a blanket for their toys.

everything

early years

Treasure baskets

Treasure baskets encourage all areas of a baby's development, and are a good way to cover all 4 areas of the **Birth to Three** Framework. Babies will play happily for lengthy periods of time, just putting the items in and out of the basket. They will love to touch and feel the different textures and experiment with the different sounds these items will make.

When planning a basket:

- Make sure the basket you are using is appropriate for the age of baby you are caring for.

- Make sure the basket is sturdy.
- Ensure the items you are using stimulate all 5 senses. Most babies explore items through touch, sight and sound but a main part of their experience will be putting objects in their mouth, so you need to make sure the objects are safe and easy to keep clean.
- Include everyday household objects and also natural objects.
- Be aware of any allergies the babies you care for may have.

What you need

- Sturdy basket.
- A range of items, you could include the following: fir cones, small tins and boxes with lids, pegs, saucepans, wooden spoons, large shells, fruit, brushes, metal spoons, keys, mirror, leather purses.

Making your treasure basket

- Place your selection of items in the treasure basket.

What to do next

Movers, Shakers and Players and *Walkers, Talkers and Pretenders*

Place the basket on the floor. If the baby is still unsteady place cushions around them so that when they reach for items they are supported. The idea of a treasure basket is for the baby to decide for themselves which objects they want to play with, and discover these without adult intervention. Your role is to observe and assist only if needed.

Whenever you put your basket out check all items, and remove and replace any damaged ones. From time to time add new items to the basket. If using the basket with an older child you could organise the contents around a single theme, for example: shiny things or wood.

everything
early years

Rattles and shakers

Babies need to be exposed to as many auditory experiences as possible. This includes listening to different types of music and sounds, and also listening to you singing and talking to them. From birth a baby can hear sounds, paying particular attention to high pitched voices. At around 5 months a baby realises where sounds come from, and will turn quickly to new sounds. At this point, the more varied the sounds and noises the more impact they will have.

Making musical instruments for a baby is a quick and easy activity which requires few items and very little adult time and input.

What you need

- Cardboard tubes, for instance: insides from kitchen rolls.
- Plastic glasses, yoghurt pots and the plastic balls used for washing liquids.
- Lentils, rice, pasta, tin milk bottle tops, small bells, shells.
- Brightly coloured sticky backed plastic or wrapping paper.
- Sticky tape, glue.
- Small amount of material.

Making your rattles and shakers

- You can make a range of different instruments using the items above. Begin by adding some lentils to an empty plastic glass or yogurt pot, now place another glass upside down on top. Tape around the edges, securing the two glasses together. You are now ready to decorate this shaker using sticky backed plastic cut into different shapes and sizes.
- To use cardboard tubes, attach some material securely to one end, using tape. Add the items you will use to make the sound to the open end, now place the material over this end and secure that with tape. Finally decorate the outside of the tube.
- Plastic washing liquid balls make lovely hand-held shakers for small hands. Fill the ball with a couple of small bells and then cover the opening using either material or sticky backed plastic. Now decorate the outside.

What to do next

Heads Up, Lookers and *Communicators* and *Sitters, Standers and Explorers*

Sit with the baby and show them what happens when they shake the rattles. Sing some of the baby's favourite songs to them using the instruments. Shake the rattles in time, introducing the baby to different rhythms. Roll the rattles along the ground for the baby who is not yet sitting up.

Movers, Shakers and Players and *Walkers, Talkers and Pretenders*

Allow the older child to pick the items they want in their rattle, and encourage them to pick it up and shake it for themselves. Teach them new nursery rhymes as they do.

everything

Scent sacks

Smell is an important sense, which most shop bought equipment and toys for young babies fail to develop. A baby actually learns to smell whilst still in the womb, and by the time it is born is able to recognise the smell of its mother's breast milk and familiar odour. These scented bags allow you to introduce your baby to a range of different and exciting smells.

What you need

- Small scrap pieces of material.
- Needle and thread.
- Ribbon.
- Washing powder tablet bags.
- A range of scents, for example: cinnamon sticks, cotton wool balls, tumble drying sheets, sheets of thin card, ribbon, vanilla essence, coffee granules, lemon essence, peppermint flavouring, small gift soaps, pot pourri, coffee granules, perfume and aftershave samples, herbs – mint, basil and lemongrass are all good for this activity. Be aware of any allergies.

Making your scent sacks

- First you need to make the bag for the scents to go in. The small bags that you place washing powder tablets in are good for this. But they can only be used for the bigger items such as cinnamon sticks and soap, because of the holes in them.
- To make your own bags, use the pattern provided (page 19). Mark and cut it out of the scrap material. Make small holes or slits where shown and thread the ribbon through. Tie both ends of the ribbon securely, when you pull the ribbon you will gather the material up and it will form a small draw-string bag.
- You are now ready to place your scented items in these bags. Items such as the cinnamon sticks, tumble drying sheets and small gift soaps can be placed straight in the bag. For items such as the essence or perfume, place drops onto the cotton wool balls and then place these in a bag.
- To use the herbs rub these over a piece of card on both sides, now fold the card and leave the herbs in the middle. Place this in the middle into the bag, the smell will last for a short time.
- If using coffee granules rub these over a slightly damp piece of card and allow them to soak in and dry before putting in the bag.

What to do next

Heads Up, Lookers and Communicators and *Sitters, Standers and Explorers*

Place these bags in a colourful container for the baby to take in and out. Sit with them and explore these scents together, sniffing the bags and then passing them to your baby. Take this opportunity to be close and snuggle with your baby. You may find they have a particular favourite scent or a scent they dislike. If possible, try using samples of perfume and aftershave that are familiar, one that their parents may use for example.

Movers, Shakers and Players and *Walkers, Talkers and Pretenders*

With an older child you can ask them questions about the smells, asking them if they like them or not.

everything

early years

Shoe box posting

Babies love to spend time posting objects in and out of slots and holes. When a baby is young he has no control over his hand and arm movements, and the only reason he will hold an object is because it is a natural reflex to grasp. But as he gets older and begins to develop, then playing with shape sorters helps hand and eye co-ordination, strengthens hand muscles, and improves fine manipulative skills when grasping, turning, placing and posting items.

What you need

- A range of empty shoe boxes.
- Wrapping paper – to decorate the boxes.
- Objects that can be used for posting, these could include: toys, spoons and other objects the baby is familiar with.

Making your post boxes

- Decorate the outside of the shoe boxes.
- Take the items you are using for posting and trace around them on to the lid of the shoe box.
- If you use the sides of the boxes as well, the shape sorter will be more difficult for older babies – as they will have to turn the boxes to find the corresponding slots.
- When drawing around the shapes, think about offsetting the items and also turning them upside down before tracing round them, so the child will have to manipulate the object to find the correct way to post it.
- Now carefully cut these shapes out.

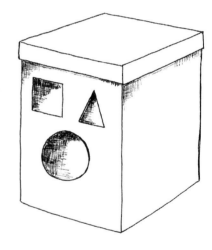

What to do next

Heads Up, Lookers and Communicators and *Sitters, Standers and Explorers*

Your boxes are now ready to be played with. Make sure the baby is sitting or lying comfortably, remember they will be leaning over to post the items if sitting up and there is a risk they may topple over, so place cushions around them for support.

Place all the items for posting on the floor in front of the boxes and begin by posting a couple through, so the baby can see what you are doing and copy you.

Movers, Shakers and Players and *Walkers, Talkers and Pretenders*

For the older child you can cut the same shapes out of a range of different boxes, so it makes it more interesting for the child and they do not only have one box to post them into. You could even colour co-ordinate boxes and pieces so the child learns to sort, for example: all the red pieces to go in the red box, and blue into the blue box.

everything

Sandwich bag books

Books play an important role in visual development and recognition; and in motor skills when turning pages. When sharing a book with you, babies have the opportunity to feel your touch, hear your voice, and examine your facial expressions and make eye contact. Most importantly, reading encourages listening and language skills – offering a baby the opportunity to babble, repeat and mimic sounds.

What you need

- Clear sandwich bags which have a running seal along the top edge.
- Bright pieces of card – the right size to fit inside the sandwich bag and sit just below the seal.
- Pictures – either drawn or cut out of magazines.
- Photos of familiar objects and people.
- Shiny coloured sweet wrappers, foil or paper.
- Dried leaves, flowers and coloured feathers.
- Glue.
- Needle and thread.

Making your sandwich bag books

- Begin by collecting together all the pictures and photos you want to use. Cut them out and mount them on bright card. Make sure you use both the front and back of your card when mounting your pictures and that the pictures are all the right way up – remember you are making a book, so the edge where the seal is will be the spine.
- Include pages that have bright patterns drawn on them, some with shiny paper and sweet wrappings, and also some with collages made from dried leaves, flowers and feathers.
- Once you have decorated all your pieces of card, and they have dried, slide them into the sandwich bags and seal them. Place all the bags on top of each other, making sure all the edges with the seals are the same way up.
- Using the needle and thread, sew along the edges of the bags just below the seal. Fasten at the end with a secure knot.

What to do next

Heads Up, Lookers and Communicators and *Sitters, Standers and Explorers*

Create a quiet cosy atmosphere for you and your baby to look at the book together. Assist in the turning of pages only if needed. Point out and name the objects and people that the baby is familiar with. Babies may find some pages more interesting than others – wanting to spend a long time looking at them, and showing no interest in others.

Movers, Shakers and Players and *Walkers, Talkers and Pretenders*

When looking at the book with an older child, allow them time to recognise and name familiar people or objects. Ask them questions about the pictures as you go along. Include a photo of the child, as they will love seeing a picture of themselves.

everything
early years

Musical mystical balloons

Babies from the age of 6 months enjoy reaching for, grasping, touching, shaking, picking up and letting go of objects. This activity not only encourages these skills, but also develops their sense of exploration and audio skills. When making these musical balloons, think about the items you are going to use and the range of noises they will make.

What you need

- A range of different coloured and shaped balloons. Think about using the long thin balloons as well as the traditional shaped ones.
- Items to put in your balloons: dried rice, shells, dried pasta, buttons, small bells, small twigs, some sugar or salt, ribbon, coloured water, balloon pump.

Making your balloons

- Begin by pulling and stretching the balloons to make it easier to blow them up.
- Add the items to the balloon. Do this by stretching the balloon neck and pushing them in, taking care not to rip the balloon.
- If using materials such as sugar, rice, flour or water then place a small funnel in the neck of the balloon. You only need to use a small amount of any of these materials.
- Once you have placed your material in the balloon, pump it up and tie it off. Do not inflate it fully, but leave it with some elasticity as this will prevent bursting.
- Once tied, add some ribbon to the balloon for the babies to use to hold the balloon when shaking it.

What to do next

Heads Up, Lookers and Communicators and Sitters, Standers and Explorers

Sit with the baby when they are exploring and playing with these balloons, showing them what happens when you shake, roll and throw the balloons. Discourage the baby from putting the balloons in their mouth. If the children find it difficult to handle and shake the balloons it may be better to tie a few balloons to a line and hang this in front of the child, so they can pat them and hit them to make noise.

Movers, Shakers and Players and Walkers, Talkers and Pretenders

When making these allow the child to choose what they want inside the balloon. For the older child encourage them to throw the balloon up into the air and catch it, the weight from the objects inside will make this easier. Talk about the different noises the different balloons make.

everything

early years

Cotton reel caterpillars

From the age of 6 months a baby is able to reach and grab for an object, using their whole hand to pass a toy from one hand to another. They develop further by moving their arms up and down together when excited. By the age of 12 months babies should be showing a preference for one hand over the other, but will still use either.

Cotton reels are the perfect size for small hands and are easy to manipulate. Making a cotton reel caterpillar will provide your child with a perfect sized piece of equipment that they will be able to pick up and play with confidently.

What you need

- Coloured shoe laces to thread through the cotton reels.
- Sticky back plastic.

Making your caterpillars

- Begin by decorating your cotton reels with the sticky back plastic.
- Now tie a knot at the end of a lace, this knot needs to be big enough not to pass through the middle of the cotton reel.
- Thread 3 cotton reels onto the lace, tie a knot the same size as before and then add another 3 reels before tying another knot. Add the final 3 reels and secure with a knot at the end. Make sure this knot is secure and that the cotton reels cannot come off.

What to do next

Heads Up, Lookers and Communicators and *Sitters, Standers and Explorers*

Sit or lay the baby on the floor and place the cotton reel caterpillar in front of them. You can encourage interest in the toy by pulling it along the ground in front of them and then by lifting it up and shaking it. Babies will try reaching for the caterpillar – developing and encouraging their gross motor skills. They will spend time passing the reels from one hand to another – looking at the colours and patterns on the reels.

If you use thick elastic to thread your reels you could stretch and attach the caterpillar across the front of a buggy or bouncy chair, giving the baby something to look at when seated.

Movers, Shakers and Players and *Walkers, Talkers and Pretenders*

When using these with the older age-group you can take the opportunity to count the number of reels and talk about the colours and patterns.

everything

early years

Puppets

Puppets are a good way to encourage many areas of development. They can help hand and eye co-ordination, fine and gross motor skills, and even develop recognition of feelings and facial expressions. They can also help with language skills – as babies like to imitate adult speech by babbling. There are a range of items that you can use to make a puppet, including a simple paper bag placed on your hand with a face drawn on it, but for this activity we are going to use old socks.

What you need

- Some old clean socks, these are better if you have a range of colours.
- Some buttons for eyes, or some plastic stick-on eyes.
- Old bits of wool for the hair.
- Needle and thread.
- Small piece of red felt to be used as a tongue.

Making your puppets

- Begin by pulling the sock onto your hand, and marking where you want to attach the eyes. Now sew the buttons on as securely as possible.
- You can now add some old wool to the top of your puppet for hair. Either stick it on or thread and knot the strands.
- Now you can attach the tongue. Put the sock on your hand and poke a small amount of it in between the gap of your fingers and thumb. This is where the mouth of your puppet will be. Mark this, remove the sock and attach a small piece of red felt as a tongue.

What to do next

Heads Up, Lookers and Communicators and Sitters, Standers and Explorers

Sit with the baby and make sure you do not scare them when first introducing the puppet. Keep it at a distance until they become familiar with it and then they will reach out to touch it themselves. Use the puppet to sing songs or tell stories, they will love to watch the movements of the puppet.

Movers, Shakers and Players and Walkers, Talkers and Pretenders

The older children can help you with making the puppet, they can choose what colour and size buttons to use for the eyes, and tell you where they want you to put them. The older children will be able to place the puppet on their hands and make it talk or make animal noises. You can use the puppets to introduce rules – talk about emotions, and even about sensitive subjects such as stranger danger or bullying.

everything
early years

Wrist rattles

From birth, babies are fascinated by their hands and fingers, and as they develop they show more and more interest in these. These wrist rattles prevent the problem of the child dropping what they are playing with, and not being able to pick it back up again. This activity promotes hand and eye co-ordination, gross motor skills and also teaches them better control over their movements.

What you need

- Strips of ribbon.
- Self-adhesive velcro.
- Small bells.
- Beads.
- Coloured thread.
- Small plastic rings.

Making your wrist rattles

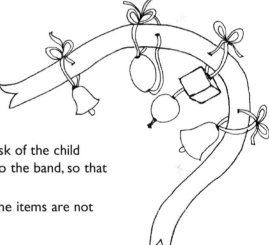

- Begin by measuring some ribbon big enough to fit around the wrist or leg of a baby. Now add some self-adhesive velcro to the ends, so it can be securely fastened around the wrist.

- Attach items to the band – by tying some strips of ribbon onto it at intervals. These should be long enough to dangle when worn by the baby, but not long enough to present a risk of the child becoming tangled up in them. Sew some beads and bells onto the band, so that when the child waves their arms the items will make noise.

- Do not over load the band with items, and make sure that the items are not too small – so there is no risk of swallowing.

What to do next

Heads Up, Lookers and Communicators and Sitters, Standers and Explorers

When the baby is wearing these rattles make sure you are with them, as their immediate reaction will be to put them in their mouths. Sit with the baby and encourage them to wave their arms and make the strands of ribbons move, making noise as they do. Another nice idea is to sit your baby in front of a mirror when they are wearing these bands and they will be able to see themselves and watch the ribbons move.

Movers, Shakers and Players and Walkers, Talkers and Pretenders

For the older child, make the strands of ribbon you attach to the bands longer, and encourage the child to move around the room waving their arms to make the ribbons move, and the bells and beads to make a noise. The older children will also enjoy watching themselves in a mirror.

Special interest cubes

Babies and young children love to pick objects up and study them; they also like stacking and building with all manner of objects. If you make a set of these interest cubes you can theme them for the baby, for example: you could make a set of animal cubes, or ones with familiar people making a range of different expressions.

You will find the template to use to make your cubes on page 20. A good idea when making these cubes is to either cover them in clear sticky back plastic, or to laminate the sheet once you have decorated it – and before you assemble it.

What you need

- Sheets of thick coloured card.
- Interesting pictures to decorate your cubes with, these can be photos, drawings or even pictures you have cut out of magazines.
- Strong glue.
- Sticky backed plastic or laminating sheets.

Making your cubes

- Begin by tracing the pattern onto sheets of card.
- Now decorate your cubes using a range of pictures.
- Once you have decorated the sheet of card, cut out the box template and score it in the appropriate places.
- Now, either cover with sticky back plastic or laminate the sheet.
- Cut out the cube and assemble it, gluing where marked.

What to do next

Heads Up, Lookers and Communicators and *Sitters, Standers and Explorers*

Sit or lay the baby comfortably on the floor, with cushions for support if needed. Place the blocks on the floor, and build a tower for them to knock over. As you pick the cubes up to build another tower, show the baby the pictures on them. Talk to the baby about the pictures, using words to name and describe them; if the pictures are of animals tell the child the noise that that animal makes.

Movers, Shakers and Players and *Walkers, Talkers and Pretenders*

The older children can help you decorate the cubes – they can choose the pictures they want to use or draw some for themselves. When using these bricks, encourage the child to build towers by stacking them, ask questions about the pictures on the bricks.

everything

early years

Crinkle and rustle packets

Hand and eye co-ordination, listening and exploring skills are all promoted through this activity. Babies develop the skill of handling and manipulating from an early age and continue to develop until they have full control over their actions. At the age of around 6 months a child can usually sit up unaided and will reach and grab for items, using their whole hand to pass an item from one hand to the other. This develops further – to using a pincer grip.

What you need

- Some scrap pieces of material.
- Needle and thread.
- Items that will make a noise: empty crisp packets (both large and small), empty chocolate box trays, sheet of brown paper, sheet of tracing paper, empty foil sweet wrappers, carrier bag.

Making your crinkle and rustle packets

- Begin by measuring the material, so it is the right size for the items going inside.
- Sew up the edges using a simple running stitch. Before you sew up the final edge put the crisp packet or paper back into the material. Sew this final edge and then your packet is finished. Continue until you have a range of packets making different noises.
- When using the plastic bag inside a packet make sure you cut it up into strips. The children should not be able to gain access to this, but if they ever did the strips will help avoid the risk of suffocation.

What to do next

Heads Up, Lookers and Communicators and *Sitters, Standers and Explorers*

Now you have made your packets sit or lay your baby comfortably and begin to play with the packets. Pick up a packet and rustle it, showing the baby what to do. Pass a packet to the baby and help them to rustle and crinkle it. The baby will soon realise what to do to make the sounds; give them time to explore the packets and the differences between them.

Movers, Shakers and Players and *Walkers, Talkers and Pretenders*

When making the packets the children can decide what pieces of material to use and what to put in each packet. When playing with the packets, use a range of words to describe the noise they are making.

Mobile template

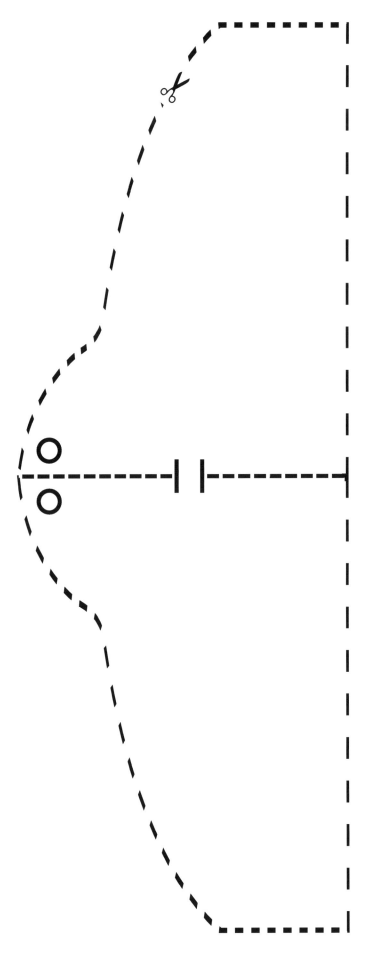

Scent sacks template

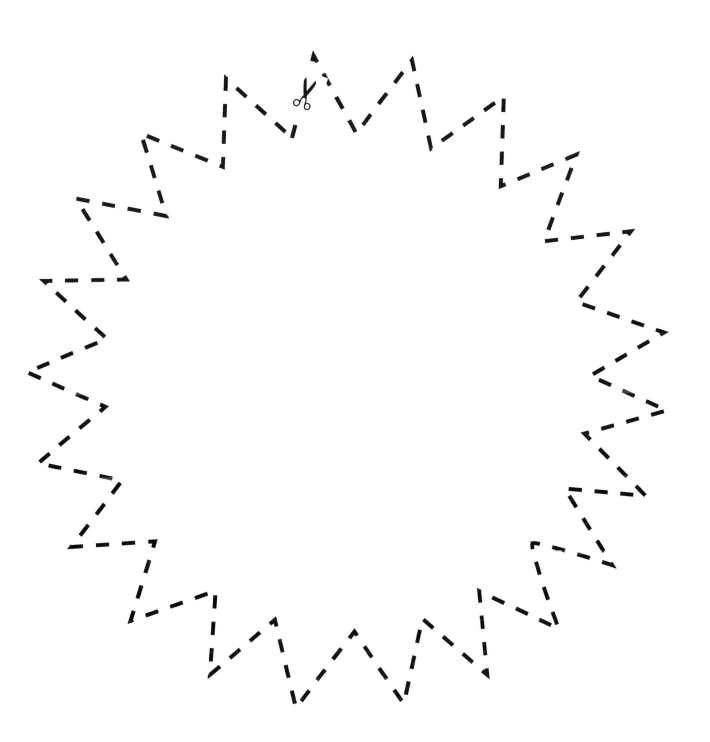

Interest cube template

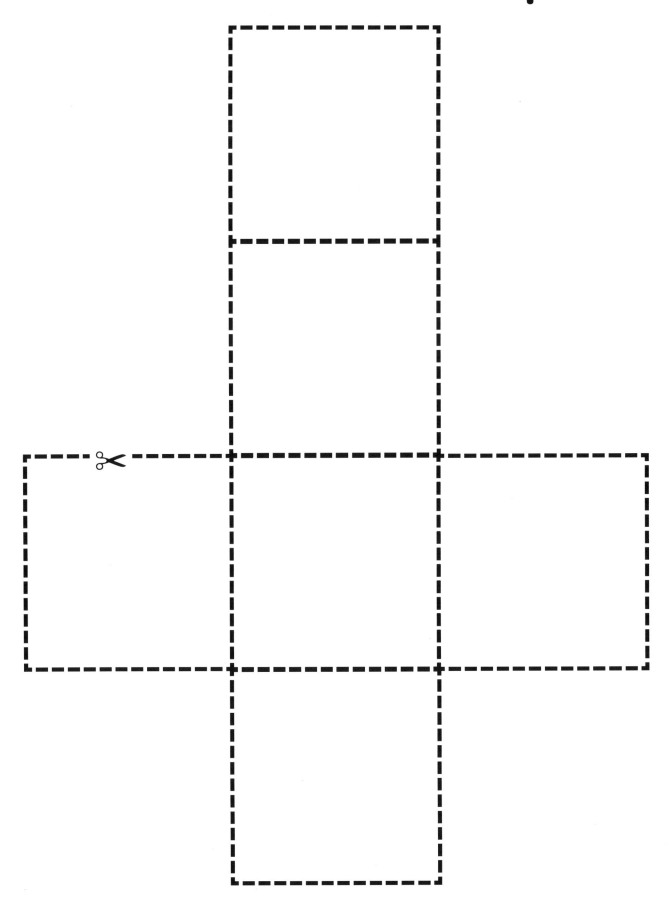